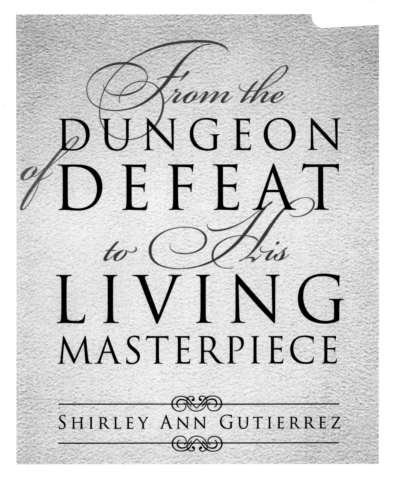

From the DUNGEON of DEFEAT to His LIVING MASTERPIECE

SHIRLEY ANN GUTIERREZ

DEDICATION

I dedicate this book to my Lord and Saviour who truly inspired me to write
The Lord and Saviour who drew me out of many waters. And Special thanks to
Cottonwood Leadership College staff as well as the students.
A special thank you to my precious son Brian Richards
A special thank you Gloria Bulthuis and Lorelei Paine for wonderful encouragement
A special thank you to Dr Charles Browning a wonderful brother in the Lord.

INTRODUCTION

These poems were written during times of when my heart was suffering
and struggling, finding myself grappling with challenges, convictions, testings,
and often shaken with fear and facing the memories of old familiar failures that haunted my soul.

From the dungeon of defeat to His living masterpiece is a book of transformation
which took place through a surrendering of the heart.

Although I had been a Christian for quite some time it was when I then made a decision
to allow for God to cleanse my heart and bring me to a place surrendering, removing/
pulling me from the muck and mire of self.

CHAINS HAVE BEEN BROKEN

Chains have been broken and the truth has set me free
Wonderful savior, mighty creator I surrender to thee
Mercy and truth preserve your name forever and ever
Jesus Christ wonderful Savior and beautiful redeemer

Wonderful Savior you have brought life to the hopeless
How sweet the sound of the angels singing
You are perfect, blameless, holy and so much more
You and only you is what my heart is searching for!!!

Yahweh, you bring out to light the shadow of death
You have conquered, you have risen
You are the God of our salvation
We cling in our hearts to the city of our destination

Behold how good and how pleasant
Is it for brothers to dwell together in unity
There is none beside you my great king
We are waiting under the shadows of your wing

I can hear the gentle voice of the spirit calling,
"Child, I pulled you from the darkness"
You've called your children to rise and step into Life
Chains have been broken because of the greatest sacrifice

Written By Shirley Gutierrez
Inspired by Jesus

Dream Weavers Dream While He Is Still King

Jesus is king while dream weavers dream,
Climbing aboard the dream weaver train
But when you're weary and feeling small
Bridge over troubled water will do nothing at all!
(Title: Dream Weaver, Song by Gary Wright)

You say it might be the night fever
Or just another brick in the wall
But it could be the last train to London
I truly tell you, Jesus is the answer to all
(Bee Gees, Pink Floyd, Electric Light Orchestra)

Did you live your life like a candle in the wind?
Never knowing who to cling to when the rain crashes in
Do not turn your back on the Lord
He is your only shelter from the storm
(Title: Candle in the Wind,
Song by: Elton John)

You can get no satisfaction but you try
This is all useless information
Triggered to fire up your imagination
Let's look to the Lord God of creation
(Title: Satisfaction, Song by: Rolling Stones)

You say you want a revolution
You tell me that it's evolution
Born to be alive is to be born again
Into the kingdom of God you will enter in
(Title: Revolution, Song by: The Beatles)

Written by Shirley Gutierrez and Various Artists
I Do Not Claim the Rights.

MATTHEW 1 : 23

They shall call His name
EMANUEL
Which being interpreted is,
GOD WITH US

GOD IS WITH US

My Heart looks at the heart of my King
And the mystery of heaven and earth
I turn to the holy commandments of God
Oh, I turn to the heart of His word

The shackles of earth you remove from my feet
You're the light in the darkness of pain
You're the first, the last, the beginning and end
For many will come in your name

You drew me out of many waters
You cast not my soul to hell
Praise Him for His mighty acts
For our God is with us now

Jesus you hold the scepter of justice
You destroy the foundations of evil
Who will awake in your likeness
Enlighten the eyes of your people

Our God who came to save the world
Praise the God of heaven and earth
I will bless His name forever and ever
O, Let us remember His marvelous works

Written by: Shirley Gutierrez
Inspired by Jesus
AUG 4, 2010

HOLY SPIRIT SPLIT DOWN THE SKIES

My spirit cries out, Holy Spirit come down
Your heart displays mountains of treasure
The earth shall shake as the heavens break at your presence
You have shown fullness of joy and rivers of pleasure

The Holy Ghost which is the way into the holiest of all
Divine and Holy Spirit come like the wind
Yahweh, Yahweh we love to see your face
Lord of all the earth, pour your spirit in this day

Bread of life let your spirit fall
Beloved Holy Spirit hear your children call
We cry Holy Spirit split the skies
Holy Spirit send us that you will be glorified

Oh God, it is good for me to draw near to you
I will praise you Lord with all of my heart
Holy Spirit come down and split the skies
Wonderful spirit, look into these hungry eyes

You are the life that fills the hunger inside
Shine your spirit as my heart cries out
You are the glory and the lifter of my head
Giver of life to these bones that were dead

Written by Shirley Gutierrez
Inspired by Jesus
5-28-2012

$\mathcal{I}$ DANCE TO THE GREAT GOD I AM

By the cross you are the truth
So we lift our hands and spin around
No longer a desolate people
We dance for the glory of the crown.

For you I will surrender my life
For You I will sing and I'll dance
For you I will show you my heart
For you I will lift up my hands

Take me to the Holy of Holies
To the throne of God, and the lamb
I will dance in the city of God
I will dance to the great God, I AM

By the blood of the king
I will dance to the lamb
I dance in your courts
To the great God, I AM

I will dance to the splendor of my king
To our Godhead, three in one
To the name above all names
The Father, the Spirit, the Son.

Written By Shirley Gutierrez
Inspired by Jesus

RETURN TO MY FIRST LOVE

I return to you Lord and set my heart on a life of understanding
Your word proclaims that you are healer of hearts and diseases of pain
Merciful, mighty, with strength and God of grace
I take your garments and remove the garments of shame

Oh, my God of Israel and healer of self inflicted wounds
Deliver my soul from a self made prison that it may awaken
You rescue your children in the day of temptation in the wilderness
Lord you have rescued me from desolation and darkness into your goodness

My God has made of one blood all nations of men to dwell on earth
The Mighty God has given to all life and breath, and all things
You have brought me out of captivity that I would be made free
Lord I have a small offering, that is me and so I lay it at your feet

My Lord is a true God and His throne is forever and ever
Magnificent wonderful king and His name is the Glorious One
The Lord has prepared a perfect blood sacrifice for the sins of the world
Redeemer and savior of the world is my Jesus his only begotten Son

Jesus you are the blood of the everlasting covenant
You are the bread of life and beloved son
My heart returns and I set my heart on a life of understanding with you
I return and repent, for I take heed to your word and walk in the truth

Written by Shirley Gutierrez ...Inspired by Jesus
Pre existing material and I do not claim the rights
Date: 2-12-2010

IN GOD I DO BELIEVE

Are we battered by the winds of change?
Are we only weak at heart?
Can we trust our one and only God?
Who's been with us from the start?

Do you believe He wants your heart?
Would you believe Him for all things?
Would you give Him everything you have?
Would you truly love your king?

Be still and know that he is God
For the Heavens and the stars He has ordained
There is No God beside my God
The Holy one of Israel is His name

I do believe He sent His Son
To die for all our sins
I do believe the cross
I do believe in Him

In spite of all my failures
He has a vision set for me
He is a God of restoration
In God I do believe.

Written By: Shirley Gutierrez
Inspired by Jesus
10-16-2011 In Honor of The Women's Support Group

JOURNEY OF PRAISE

ISAIAH 61 : 1

The Spirit of the Sovereign LORD is on me, because the LORD has anointed me to preach good news to the poor. He has sent me to bind up the brokenhearted, to proclaim Freedom for the captives and release from Darkness for the prisoners

In darkness pain and suffering
Would you look to the altar of souls
Oh, turn your heart to the martyr
Oh, turn your heart to those

You're acquainted with their suffering
The roads they've never known
Turn to those and touch them
For the glory of your throne

Lifting up their faces
Established in the faith
As they walk the fields of hunger
For the journey of your praise

Your mercies shall compass their journey
They speak as oracles of you
They are made to stand for battle
They are made to stand for truth

From persecution and affliction
To the fifth seal and to a white robe
The revelation of Jesus Christ
The lamb who takes the scroll

Written by: Shirley Gutierrez

LOOKING TO YOU

I've climbed the walls of Egypt
I've rolled with the seas
I've covered the distance
My God living in me

I'm laying down my life
I'm reaching the view
I'm crossing the mainline
Yes, I'm looking to you.

I'm climbing the mountains
I'm crashing the seas
You've broken the chains Lord
The Wind is running with me.

I'm running to your cross
Yes I'm looking to you
I'm seeking your ways
I'm seeking your truth

I'm reaching for your arms
And I'm calling my king
I'm looking to heaven
And he's looking to me.

Written By: Shirley Gutierrez

 ASTER OF MERCY

Meet me in the early morning splendor Lord
Where stillness bows to your glory
Mercy and truth preserve your name
In the beauties of holiness from the womb of the morning

My heart is my devotion to you
I bring you my mind for rest and renewal
You are the gold mine of peace deep within
Waiting to be trapped again and again

Great is the Lord and greatly to be praised
A love with an eternal grip on me
I will burn the midnight oil in pursuit of you
As you are the master of mercy and master of truth

Power and healing are in your name
You keep me as the apple of your eye
You hide me under the shadow of your wings
You brought me out as I was bound with chains

My life is no longer subject to the whims
Of a sin stained deity
As your love has torn down these walls
So shall your strength overcomes those that fall

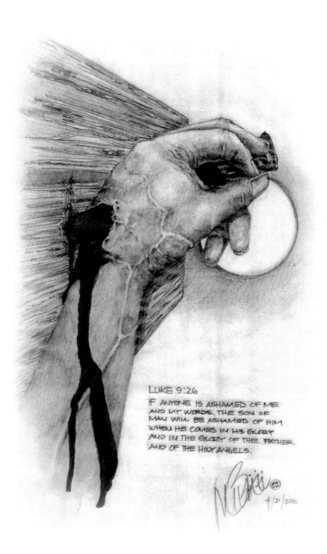

LUKE 9:26
IF ANYONE IS ASHAMED OF ME
AND MY WORDS, THE SON OF
MAN WILL BE ASHAMED OF HIM
WHEN HE COMES IN HIS GLORY
AND IN THE GLORY OF THE FATHER
AND OF THE HOLY ANGELS.

4/21/2006

My Great Pain For
The Glory of the King

Lord this world of damnation is badgering at my heart
Shall I speak in the anguish of my spirit or bitterness of my soul?
How long will the spirit of the afflicted swallow injustice?
Will the lacerations of the heart become foreign and gross?

This flesh is swallowed up in a sea of trouble
How long will I eat the bread of sorrow?
Wounds of my world shuttle without hope
My face is foul with weeping like that of Job

Fear and trembling have made my bones to shake
The perverse fixations of hearts waxed cold
Why have they plunged my heart to suffering?
My great pain for the Glory of the King

I ran away from my God who waited patiently for me
While on every side I was destroyed and gone
And my hope they removed like a tree
But it was God who came to save me

I will esteem the words of my God
As you have enlarged me when I was in distress
You are my God that has mercy upon me
My great pain will bring glory to our king.

Written by: Shirley Gutierrez Inspired by The Lord Jesus Christ
8-02-2011

SWEET WHISPERS

I whisper of my love for you
As I make your heart my home
Sweet whispers in your garden Lord
Sweet whispers in your throne

I whisper to your heart, O God
I whisper to my king
I whisper all my troubles Lord
And I whisper all good things

I whisper in your stillness Lord
O, I whisper to your soul
Give me details of your heart
I have one cause to know

I whisper, I exalt you Lord
As I'm sitting by your side
My delight is in your love
I whisper you're my prize.

King David whispered to your heart
While you whisper to my thoughts
You whisper grace and mercy
And I whisper you're my God.

Written By: Shirley Gutierrez
Inspired By Jesus

THE LOVE OF JESUS CHRIST

LUKE 19 :10

For the Son of Man came to Seek and Save the Lost

You stretch the sky above all things
A clue of where You are
You came with values deep and strong
To purify and sanctify our hearts

You navigate my heart, oh God
As your Son's life patterns me
You have no quantity of love
A love of no degree

My thoughts, my heart, my love for you
For the grace you've given me
Remove all things that don't belong
Your truth will set us free

You've given me remission Lord
A sweet abundant life
The weight of all the world
Was laid on Jesus Christ

My love is amplified for you
And your noble qualities
I hold your heart in high esteem
I pay homage to my king

WRITTEN BY: SHIRLEY GUTIERREZ
INSPIRED BY: JESUS CHRIST
5-31-2010

THE CITY OF
THE GREAT DEFENDER

An entrance into the city of heaven
Streets of gold as clear as crystal
In the city of the true great defender
The Son, the great and beautiful redeemer

Strength and beauty are in the presence of the healer
There he was clothed with a vesture dipped in blood
A dwelling place where my soul abides
A furnace of hearts of the purified

His name is called the word of God
The armies which were in heaven followed him
Upon white horses, clothed in fine linen, white and clean
And on His thigh a name is written, KING OF KINGS

Let us build ourselves in the most holy faith
In the image of the son of God and the God of grace
Blessed are they which are called into the marriage
supper of the lamb
Into the city of the Son of God of the great God I AM

He said unto the one, it is done
I am the alpha and omega, the beginning and end
To the thirsty I will give the Fountain of Life
Great victories, I give to the children of the Lord Jesus Christ.

Written By: Shirley Gutierrez
Inspired by Jesus
Pre-existed Material and I do not claim the rights
03-03-12

THE HOPE OF GLORY
HOLDING YOUR HAND

The power of darkness released in the night
Terror and affliction kissing their deeds
Hell and destruction preparing the way
Satan's desire for you and for me

Paralyzed in anguish, sorrow and shame
Fenced in darkness where vile spirits remain
Trade in your sorrows, trade in your shame
Die to your flesh to a life you will gain

Who holds the fear that makes you afraid?
He that is mighty conquered the grave
A self made prison of grief and despair
For God is the light, my heart will declare

He sprinkles you clean then gives you a heart
He gives you a spirit to walk in His ways
He satisfies richly and gives you true life
Breaking the chains from darkness to light

Look not to the world that is tainted with sin
The plans for your life is in the hands of your God
The hope of glory is holding your hand
The journey, the vision, our Christ and His plan

Written by Shirley Gutierrez
Inspired by Jesus Christ
* Pre existing material and not claiming rights

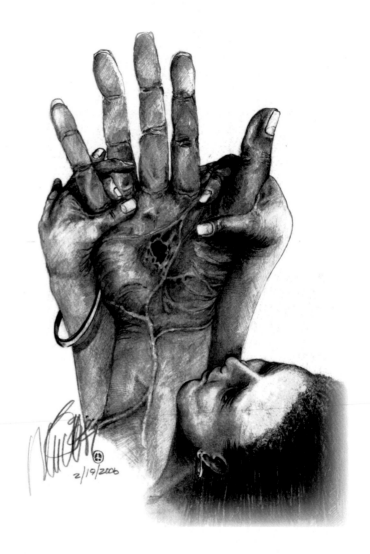

THE SPIRIT AND THE BRIDE SAY COME

Our roots wax cold my Lord
Our bones are weak and dry
Give us healing water
O breath, make us alive

Cast your spirit upon us Lord
To preach among the living
Your everlasting gospel
In streets of every city

You prepare us for the nations
You lift our hearts to you
Wake up your mighty people
With one cause for the truth

You fill the face of the world
The fruit that bears you glory
You offer living water
Your mercies ever pouring

KING OF KINGS AND LORD OF LORDS
A bright and morning star before me
The spirit and the bride say come
Living waters pouring

Written By Shirley Gutierrez
Inspired by Jesus

1 JOHN 5:5
AND WHO CAN WIN THIS BATTLE
AGAINST THE WORLD? ONLY THOSE
WHO BELIEVE THAT JESUS IS THE
SON OF GOD. •NLT•

TIE YOUR HEARTS TO THE GOD OF AMERICA

Oh, tie your hearts to the God of America
Oh lift your eyes to the bright and morning star
Let the rivers clap their hands, let the mountains sing
As the people clasp their hearts to the everlasting king

Give unto the Lord the glory due unto His name
Oh, Give thanks to the God of heaven and earth
Praise the works of God for they will stand
Lift high the Kings of Kings and the great I am.

In His hands are the deep places of the earth
In His heart are the deep places of His thoughts
Praise him ye mountains and hills, and all ye fruitful trees
Let us magnify the God of America and everlasting king

A land which has foundations, whose builder and maker is God
Lord you have been our dwelling place in all generations
You have guided your people in your strength unto your holy habitation
O, Lord we tie our hearts to you in humble admiration

Sick, lame, near and far
There's redemption for every heart
Every nation, tribe and tongue
Exalt the king and join as one.

Written By: Shirley Gutierrez
Inspired By: Jesus
4-7-2012
Pre- Existing Material and I do not claim the rights (Scripture # 3, 4)

WE ARE WAITING HERE

Your daughters and your sons
We are waiting here
Looking to your kingdom
Our banquet day is near

The view of our beloved
Clasping our hearts to the king
Yes your children waiting
Under the shadows of your wing

A sweet taste to my heart
A taste of heavens fire
The Alpha, the Omega
The throne of our Messiah

A beauty of his revelation
As the King of Kings appears
The promise of our Savior
The appointed day is here

Embracing your arrival Lord
Captured by your sight
Glory streaming from your face
And heaven in your eyes.

Written By Shirley Gutierrez
Inspired by Jesus

WORLD, DON'T GO SILENT

I ponder of you with great thoughts
I cannot keep silent concerning my king
I'm amazed at your wonderful love for all is pleasant
A wonderful love that is not silent to me

I ponder of your plan to reason with us
All generations let us stand and rise
I cry we cannot be silent concerning my king
I cry and let us speak out of our Christ

The ways of the world grow silent
As he holds a world of mercy for me
I will sing out to Him in triumph
I give my heart to Jesus a living offering

His grace speaks in the thunder of lightning
His mercies are not silent toward me
His grace cries out to the world
As he points to the cross and the tree

The heart of this king is unfathomable
To proclaim the name of my savior and king
As I desire to preach the living word
To proclaim the name of my savior and king

To silence the word of my God, for my heart will never agree
Holy God I turn to my knees
Let not your hearts be silent
Oh, children of God let not this true love die

Written By Shirley Gutierrez
Inspired by Jesus

JOHN 14:6
JESUS ANSWERED
"I AM THE WAY AND THE TRUTH
AND THE LIFE", ...

A special thank you to Mike Filitti for the illustrations used in this book

To order additional copies of this book, contact:
Xlibris
1-888-795-4274
www.Xlibris.com
Orders@Xlibris.com

Print information available on the last page

Rev. date: 11/19/2019

Printed in the United States
By Bookmasters